ROOTED & READY:
A CAMP STAFF DEVOTIONAL FOR BOLD FAITH AND SELFLESS SERVICE

JAMES MCLAMB

Rooted & Ready: A Camp Staff Devotional for Bold Faith and Selfless Service

Copyright © 2025 by James McLamb

All rights reserved.

Publisher Information
James McLamb/Generation Youth
Raleigh, North Carolina

For more information or to contact the author, please visit generation-youth.com or email james@generationziglar.com.

ISBN 979-8-89165-255-2 (softcover)

Cover design: Abigael Elliott
Cover photo credit: TBD
Interior design: eBookBurner Technologies
First printing: 2025
Printed in the United States of America

DEDICATION

To Camp Caraway—where my calling was confirmed and my heart for youth took root.

Those college summers were filled with early mornings, late-night laughter, and life-changing moments that still echo in my soul. This book was shaped by the sacred ground where I first learned what it truly means to serve.

 # INTRODUCTION

WHY I WROTE THIS DEVOTIONAL

Camp changed my life.

Not just because of the laughter around the campfire or the late-night talks with campers. Not just because of the lifelong friendships formed over popsicle sticks and bunk inspections. But because God used those weeks—those intense, beautiful, exhausting, joy-filled weeks—to shape my heart, stretch my faith, and grow me into the kind of person I had prayed to become.

I served full-time on summer camp staff in college. It was hot, messy, and humbling. It was also sacred.

Through the rhythms of rising early, leading devotions, plunging into dish duty, and praying over campers before lights out, I experienced something far deeper than a summer job. I saw how God could use an ordinary college student—me—to love others in extraordinary ways. I saw how God was just as interested in growing me as He was in reaching the kids I was assigned to lead.

Over the years, I've served in all kinds of camp settings:

- As a counselor, leaning into one-on-one discipleship

- As a camp speaker, preaching truth and encouraging surrender

- And now, for many years, as someone who trains and equips camp staffs across the country

And it's not just *my* story.

My wife served as a summer counselor during her college years. She'll tell you it was one of the most spiritually refining times of her life. And now, all three of our children have served on summer camp staffs too. Watching them pour out their lives, wrestle with Scripture, rely on grace, and walk shoulder to shoulder with other young leaders—it only deepened my conviction:

☞ There is something uniquely powerful about what God does in the life of a young adult during camp ministry.

So after years of leading, observing, laughing, crying, and praying with camp staffs, I began to see a pattern—certain values, certain heart-postures, that marked the most impactful staffers. They weren't perfect. But they were rooted in Christ. And they were ready to serve.

That's where this devotional comes from.

It's not a manual for perfect camp performance. It's a 14 devotional daily guide for spiritual growth—for becoming the kind of leader God can use to change lives, including your own.

This is for the staffer who is hungry for more than just surviving summer.

This is for the leader who wants to grow in faith, character, and purpose.
This is for the one who feels both excited and unsure—and wants to be reminded that they were called here on purpose.

In the pages that follow, you'll find 12 core values—single words that capture what it means to lead like Jesus in a camp setting. These aren't just theories; they're truths I've seen lived out over decades. Truths I've seen take root in college students who arrived with questions and left transformed.

If you let Him, God will use this summer to do more than impact your campers—
He'll use it to refine your heart, expand your vision, and deepen your relationship with Him.

So here we go.
You're not just showing up for a job.
You're stepping into a calling.

Let's get rooted.
Let's get ready.

—James

CALLED FOR A PURPOSE

Scripture – 2 Timothy 1:9 (ESV):
"who saved us and called us to a holy calling, not because of our works but because of his own purpose and grace, which he gave us in Christ Jesus before the ages began"

I'll never forget the moment it all clicked.

It was the end of our seventh day of staff training. The sun had set, the fireflies were out, and a damp summer breeze was settling over the campgrounds. Most of us were sitting on picnic tables, some on the ground, just outside the dining hall. Seven full days of orientation, team-building, training sessions, cabin prep, worship services, schedule run-throughs, and spiritual challenges had left us physically exhausted and mentally overloaded—but also quietly energized.

It had been a whirlwind.

We'd scrubbed toilets, memorized camp policies, practiced counselor skits, and even rehearsed emergency procedures. We learned how to guide small groups, how to care for homesick campers, and how to stay alert during late-night cabin duty.

I was 20. Young. Idealistic. Eager to serve.
But I'll admit, I also wondered if I was in over my head.

That night, with our training week almost behind us, a group of us gathered together to debrief. Some of us were laughing about the chaos of campfire practice. Others were quietly admitting we were nervous about being responsible for a dozen kids just days from now. We passed around stories, snacks, and honest questions.

And then—one of the senior counselors spoke up. A quiet guy with a presence about him. The kind of guy you paid attention to when he did speak.

"You guys realize something, right?" he said, leaning forward slightly.

"They're not just training us to be great counselors... they're showing us how to be better Christians."

Silence.
Then slow nods.
It hit us.

🎯 MORE THAN A JOB

That sentence has echoed in my heart for years now.
At the time, it reframed everything.

You see, up until that moment, I had seen staff training as a boot camp for youth ministry logistics—learning how to keep kids safe, energized, and engaged. And yes, that's part of it. But that night, I realized something deeper was happening beneath the surface.

The camp directors weren't just handing us rules and routines—they were laying a spiritual foundation. They weren't just coaching us to survive summer; they were calling us to be *formed* in Christ.

All the little things—the way we were taught to wake up early with purpose, to serve without being asked, to treat everyone as valuable, to pray constantly, and to forgive quickly—these weren't just good camp practices. They were kingdom practices.

They were preparing us for something *bigger than camp*.

They were preparing us to walk in the holy calling God had placed on our lives.

YOU'RE NOT JUST HERE TO WORK

You didn't end up at this camp on accident.

Maybe it started with a job application. Maybe a friend invited you. Maybe you just needed something to do this summer, or felt a tug you couldn't explain. But however you got here—God *appointed* this moment. You are here because you were *called*.

2 Timothy 1:9 makes it clear:
You were called to a **holy calling**, not because of your impressive qualifications, but because of **His purpose and grace.**

Let that settle in for a moment.

This summer is more than a job. It's a divine appointment. It's a sacred assignment.

It's not just about managing a cabin or leading fun activities.

It's about becoming the person God has called you to be—for these campers, this team, this time.

 ## A HOLY CALLING

What does a *holy calling* look like at camp?

It's showing up with joy, even when you're tired.
It's giving grace to a camper who's testing your patience.
It's being the first to serve and the last to complain.
It's praying before a difficult conversation.
It's owning your mistakes and learning from them.
It's pointing campers to Jesus—not just with your words, but with your example.

This kind of calling will stretch you. It will push you to the end of yourself.
But that's exactly where God wants to meet you.

In fact, I've learned something in all my years speaking at camps and training staff:

☞ Camp is a classroom for character.
God will use this summer to expose the areas where you need to grow, and then—through community, worship, trials, and victories—He'll gently shape you into someone more like Jesus.

And the amazing thing is, while God is shaping you... He's also using you to shape others.

YOU'RE PART OF A BIGGER STORY

Maybe you don't feel ready.
Maybe you're wondering if you'll be a good counselor, or worrying that you don't know the Bible well enough, or that you won't have the right words in hard moments.

Let me tell you something I've told dozens of staff members over the years:

God isn't looking for perfect people—He's looking for willing ones.

The truth is, most of your campers won't remember your small group outlines.
They'll remember the way you listened.
They'll remember your laugh, your patience, your kindness when they messed up.
They'll remember the way you lived like Jesus.

And that starts with recognizing this:
You've been called.
You've been equipped.
You are exactly where God wants you.

 **REFLECT**

Take 10–15 minutes to sit quietly with God today. Reflect on these questions—write them in your journal, or talk them out with a teammate.

- How did you end up at camp this summer? Looking back, can you see God's hand in your story?
- What are you most excited about? What are you most nervous about?
- What does it mean to you personally to be "called to a holy calling"?
- In what ways do you hope God shapes your faith this summer?

 **PRAYER**

Father, thank You for calling me. Thank You for placing me exactly where You want me this summer. Help me not to see this role as just another thing to do, but as a holy opportunity to grow in You, to serve others, and to reflect Jesus to everyone I meet. Give me the strength, humility, and joy I need for the journey ahead. Make me ready—rooted in Your truth, anchored in Your love, and bold in my calling. In Jesus' name, amen.

SERVANTHOOD

Scripture – Mark 10:45 (ESV):
"For even the Son of Man came not to be served but to serve, and to give his life as a ransom for many."

I had no idea what I had signed up for.

It was my first official day as a camp counselor, and I stood at the edge of the cabin porch watching the first wave of campers emerge from the trees. I had been through a full week of staff training, filled with worship, learning, and preparation. I felt confident... or at least prepared. That confidence, however, started to crack the moment I laid eyes on my assigned campers.

There were four boys in my first cabin group—middle schoolers, somewhere between 12 and 13 years old. I expected them to be quirky, energetic, and maybe even a little awkward. What I didn't expect was the complete unpredictability of what was walking toward me.

One was 6'3"—taller than me by at least half a foot—and already had the build of a high school basketball player.
The second? A hefty guy, easily over 100 pounds heavier than my 145-pound frame, huffing up the trail while his duffel bag bulged with what looked like a month's supply of snacks and mismatched socks.
Then came a kid hauling not one, not two, but five bags—as if he'd mistaken a week-long camp for a full semester abroad.
And the last? Barely 5' tall, with a shaved head and a lone rat tail flowing in the wind like a rebellious flag of independence.

They were loud.
They were unpredictable.
They were all completely different—and they all had needs I hadn't anticipated.

Before that day was over, I had to coordinate behavioral medications, figure out how to split up beds to avoid arguments, and clean up after one of the boys had wet the bed in the middle of the night. There were power struggles over snack rations, complaints about the food, tears over homesickness, and no shortage of "He said—No I didn't— Yes you did!" battles in the cabin.

I remember collapsing onto my bunk late that night, whispering to God, *"Why am I here?"*

That's when I first began to understand that camp counseling wasn't just about leadership—it was about **servanthood**.

LEADERSHIP STARTS LOW

In Mark 10:45, Jesus makes a radical statement to His disciples:
"For even the Son of Man came not to be served but to serve, and to give his life as a ransom for many."

Let's be clear—if anyone deserved to be served, it was Jesus. He was the Messiah. The King of Kings. The Creator of the universe walking in human flesh. But instead of demanding worship or insisting on status, He wrapped a towel around His waist, got down on His knees, and washed His disciples' feet. He chose the posture of a servant.

And then He told us to go and do the same.

Servanthood is not glamorous.
It's not always appreciated.
It's not often acknowledged.
And it definitely doesn't go viral on social media.

But it's the posture of Jesus. And it's the foundation of what makes a camp counselor truly great.

 ## SERVANTHOOD LOOKS LIKE THIS...

Servanthood at camp means replacing sheets at 1:00 a.m. because your camper had an accident and is too embarrassed to ask for help.

It means catching a quiet kid in the back of the group and slowing your pace so he doesn't feel invisible.

It means getting up earlier than everyone else so you can pray over your campers before they even open their eyes.

It means sitting out of the fun sometimes so a homesick camper doesn't sit alone.

It means biting your tongue when a camper talks back... again.

It means doing the little things with great love—especially when no one's watching.

WHY IT'S SO HARD (AND SO HOLY)

Let's be honest—serving others isn't natural. Everything in our culture screams, *"Make it about you!"* Be seen. Be important. Be respected. Be in control.

But Jesus flips that script. In His Kingdom, the greatest one is the servant of all. That means leadership at camp doesn't start with popularity or performance—it starts with a towel in hand and a heart surrendered.

The first few days of camp may stretch you beyond anything you expected. You may already feel it. You might be wondering if you can handle it all—if you're strong enough, spiritual enough, patient enough.

Good.

Because that's where God begins to work. When you realize your strength isn't enough, you begin to lean into His.

God didn't bring you here because you were already enough. He brought you here to make you more like His Son.

THE POWER OF PRESENCE

Here's something I've learned through years of leading and training staff: most campers won't remember your name five years from now.

But they'll remember the way you made them feel.
They'll remember that you were kind when they were melting down.
That you sat with them when they were afraid.
That you didn't laugh when they cried.
That you made them feel seen, known, and loved.

That's servanthood. That's ministry. That's Christ in you, shining through.

 ## FROM YOU TO THEM—AND BACK AGAIN

Here's the beauty of it all: while you're pouring out your time, your energy, your strength—God is pouring something into you.

Every time you serve when you don't feel like it...
Every time you choose patience over pride...
Every time you get low so someone else can be lifted up...

You're being shaped.

You're not just doing ministry—you're becoming someone who embodies the heart of Jesus.

That night, when I laid on my bunk, exhausted and unsure, I didn't yet realize that God was answering a prayer I hadn't even prayed out loud: *"God, make me more like You."*

 **REFLECT**

Take some time today—alone or with your journal—and consider:

- In what ways have you already been challenged to serve this week?
- How do you typically respond when serving becomes inconvenient or unnoticed?
- What would it look like to *embrace* servanthood, even in the most frustrating moments?

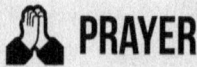 **PRAYER**

Jesus, thank You for showing me what true leadership looks like. Help me to serve like You—with humility, love, and joy. When I'm tired, remind me that You are my strength. When I want to be seen, remind me that You see me. Make me more like You through the way I serve others. I surrender my pride, my comfort, and my plans—use me however You want this week. Amen.

UNITY

Scripture – Ephesians 4:3 (ESV):
"eager to maintain the unity of the Spirit in the bond of peace."

There's something sacred about a group of people pulling in the same direction, with the same heart, toward the same purpose.

I experienced that kind of unity for the first time as a college student on summer camp staff.

We were an all-male staff, just barely enough of us to make the camp run. We were outnumbered by campers, overworked, and under-rested. There were more chores than we had hands to do them. The schedule never stopped. The campers didn't always cooperate. The days were long and the nights were short.

But somehow—through the sweat, the strain, the early mornings and the late-night prayers—something beautiful happened.

We became family.

We learned each other's strengths, covered for each other's weaknesses, and learned to laugh through the chaos. We bore each other's burdens in the most literal ways—whether it was scrubbing dishes together, leading devotions, dragging a homesick camper up a hill, or praying side by side at the end of a hard day.

There were no superstars. No one was trying to stand out. We were just brothers on a mission—to make Jesus known, to serve our campers well, and to carry each other when we got tired.

And we did get tired.

But we didn't quit.
Because we weren't doing it alone.

🫶 UNITY DOESN'T JUST HAPPEN

Ephesians 4:3 tells us to be *"eager to maintain the unity of the Spirit in the bond of peace."*

That word *"eager"* matters.

Unity doesn't happen by accident. It doesn't fall into your lap just because you wear the same t-shirt or attend the same training. Unity takes effort. It takes intention. It takes *fighting for peace*—not with fists, but with humility, grace, and love.

Unity means stepping in when a teammate is struggling, even if your plate is full.
It means holding your tongue when you're frustrated.
It means praying instead of gossiping.
It means trusting each other, forgiving quickly, and choosing to believe the best.

It means realizing that the person next to you is not your competition—they're your co-laborer.

You cannot lead well if you don't link arms.

Because the truth is, campers can feel the difference.
A divided staff will lead divided cabins.
But a united staff? That's a force for the Gospel that no summer storm or schedule change can shake.

WHEN BROTHERHOOD BECOMES A FOUNDATION

I didn't fully realize the impact of that first summer until much later.

Many of the guys I served with that year are still my friends—thirty years later. We've stood in each other's weddings. We've called each other in moments of celebration and heartbreak. And more than anything, we've stayed connected because we shared something eternal: the bond of Christ, forged through selfless service.

I think about those men often.

They didn't just model how to run a great camp—they modeled what it looks like to live out the Gospel. I watched them lead with *joy,* even when they were bone-tired. I watched them walk in *humility,* not needing credit for the hard work they did. And I watched them choose *integrity,* especially when it would've been easier to cut corners.

Those three traits—joy, humility, and integrity—formed the foundation of my spiritual life in a way no classroom ever could.

They weren't preaching sermons with microphones, but they preached daily with their lives.

And week after week, as we knelt beside bunk beds and cleaned up cabins and gathered around the final night's campfire, I could feel something greater than any of us pulling us together.

ONE IN THE SPIRIT, ONE IN THE LORD

Every Friday night, we would gather around the fire for our final worship of the week. Campers lined the benches, counselors stood behind them, and the crackle of the flames danced under a canopy of stars.

And we'd sing:

> *We are one in the Spirit, we are one in the Lord.*
> *We are one in the Spirit, we are one in the Lord.*
> *And we pray that all unity may one day be restored.*

*And they'll know we are Christians by our love, by our
love,*
Yes, they'll know we are Christians by our love.

That song never left me.

Decades later, I can still hear it—can still feel it. That chorus
became a kind of anthem, not just for our camp, but for how
we understood our mission.

We weren't just counselors.
We weren't just guys with matching shirts and schedules.
We were *brothers in Christ,* united by the Holy Spirit, and
called to reflect the love of Jesus to every single camper.

We were one.

And our unity was the loudest sermon we preached all
summer.

🛠 BUILDING UNITY WHERE YOU ARE

You don't need to wait for unity to magically show up. You
get to help build it.

And unity doesn't mean uniformity. You don't all have to
think the same, look the same, or lead the same way. But you
do have to *love* the same way—with the love of Christ.

Here's how you fight for unity on your staff:

- **Pray for your teammates.** Especially the ones that
  challenge you.

- Celebrate each other's wins. Resist the urge to compare.

- Ask for help. Vulnerability builds trust.
- Serve without being asked. Show up for each other in small ways.
- Speak truth with grace. Don't let bitterness fester—deal with it in love.
- Worship together. Nothing unites hearts faster than shared surrender.

The campers won't always see your planning or your preparation—but they *will* see how you treat each other. That may be the clearest picture of Christ they get all week.

○ LET LOVE SPEAK LOUDEST

I believe with all my heart that the Gospel travels best on the rails of unity. Jesus even prayed in John 17 that His followers would be one—*so that the world would believe.*

That's still true today.

Your unity is a testimony.
Your love is a witness.
Your brotherhood (and sisterhood) in Christ may speak louder than anything you say.

So when the schedule breaks down, when personalities clash, when tension creeps in—remember this:
Unity is worth fighting for.
Because Jesus fought for it first.

REFLECT

Spend a few moments reflecting on these questions. If you're journaling or sitting with a small group, talk them through honestly:

- Who on your team are you most grateful for right now? Have you told them?
- Are there any conflicts or tensions that need healing in your relationships?
- What small actions can you take today to build unity?

PRAYER

Lord, thank You for giving me a team to serve with this summer. Help me to pursue unity—not just in easy moments, but especially when things get hard. Give me a heart that forgives quickly, serves eagerly, and loves deeply. May our staff be known by our love. Make us one in the Spirit, one in You. In Jesus' name, amen.

JOY

Scripture – Philippians 4:4 (ESV):
"Rejoice in the Lord always; again I will say, rejoice."

There's something about the early weeks of camp that feels electric.

Everyone is fresh off training, hopeful, energized, and ready to make a difference. The sun is shining, the campers are wide-eyed, and even the daily schedule feels like an adventure.

But somewhere in week four—or five, or six—that shine begins to wear off.

Counselors get tired. Bodies start aching from late nights and long days. Patience runs thin. The music you once sang with passion now feels repetitive. You've told the same story to five different cabin groups and answered the same camper questions over and over again. You wonder if what you're doing is even making a difference.

That's where I was one particular summer—about halfway through the season. Our staff had grown quiet, shoulders slouched just a little more than usual. We weren't in crisis; we were just worn out.

And then Gordon showed up.

 ## THE UNEXPECTED SPARK

Gordon was a college friend to many of us, a guy who had grown up in a missionary family serving overseas. That week, he came to serve in a special role—a "camp missionary"— someone who would speak at chapel and share how God was working around the world.

Each week we had a new missionary come in, and most of them gave meaningful updates: photos from distant countries, stories of orphanages, testimonies of God's faithfulness in hard places. These moments reminded us that we were part of something bigger, and they always helped campers grasp the importance of the Great Commission.

But when Gordon arrived, he brought more than stories. He brought *joy.*

And not just the laugh-at-everything kind of joy. Not just positive vibes or forced happiness. Gordon had a *contagious, deep-rooted joy* that lit up every room he stepped into.

He smiled big, served humbly, and laughed freely. But what made Gordon different wasn't his energy—it was his focus.

He didn't just talk *about* God.
He walked *with* God.
And you could see it in everything he did.

THE SOURCE OF JOY

As the week went on, I found myself watching Gordon—not just when he was on stage, but in the in-between moments. He'd sit with campers, ask intentional questions, and listen well. He prayed for staff before chapel. He helped set up games and encouraged kids during field activities like it was his personal mission to make everyone feel seen.

One day during staff lunch, someone finally asked him, "Man, how do you have so much energy? Don't you ever get tired?"

He smiled, leaned forward, and simply said,
"I do get tired. But my joy doesn't come from how I feel. My joy comes from who God is."

That hit me like a brick.

In Philippians 4:4, Paul doesn't just tell us to rejoice. He tells us to *"Rejoice in the Lord always."* Not *sometimes.* Not *when the campers listen.* Not *when the weather's perfect.* But *always.*

Joy, according to Scripture, is more than an emotion—it's a choice.
And not just a choice to smile, but a choice to *focus on God.*

That week, Gordon helped us realign.
He reminded us that Christian joy is:

- Rooted in the character and promises of God, not in how things are going.

- Sustained by God's love, grace, and faithfulness, not our personal strength.

- Found in God's presence and anchored in belief (see 1 Peter 1:8).

🧠 WHEN THE FUN FADES

Let's be honest—camp is fun. Most of the time.

But when joy starts slipping away, we usually try to fix it by *adding more fun.*
More games. More caffeine. More jokes.
But real joy isn't something you manufacture. It's something you cultivate.

Gordon didn't bring joy by being silly—he brought it by being rooted.

He made time to be in God's Word each morning.
He prayed constantly, not as a duty, but as a rhythm.
He thanked God out loud for the little things—a camper's breakthrough moment, a cool breeze during chapel, a successful small group.
He served others without complaint.
He smiled even when he was drenched in sweat.
And through it all, he reminded us that *joy is not about the absence of stress—it's about the presence of Jesus.*

🌿 CULTIVATING JOY IN CAMP LIFE

Here's what I've learned over the years: if you don't intentionally protect your joy, the grind of summer will quietly steal it.

Here are a few ways you can cultivate deep, Christ-centered joy this week:

🔅 1. FOCUS ON GOD

Joy comes from closeness with Him. Start and end your day with prayer, even if it's short. Reflect on His faithfulness in Scripture. Remember who you're serving—and why.

🙌 2. PRACTICE GRATITUDE

Make a habit of noticing small blessings. Thank God for them. Gratitude waters the soil where joy grows.

🌳 3. ABIDE IN CHRIST

Stay connected to Jesus—not just when you lead devotions or during chapel, but throughout your day. Lean on His strength. Obey His voice.

👉 4. SERVE OTHERS

When joy feels distant, try shifting your focus from yourself to someone else. Encourage a teammate. Pray over a camper. Serve without needing thanks.

🤝 5. STAY IN COMMUNITY

Share the highs and lows with your team. Laugh together. Worship together. Remind each other of truth when someone's joy is running low.

🎵 "THEY'LL KNOW WE ARE CHRISTIANS..."

That summer, when we gathered around the fire on Friday night, something was different. The staff was still tired—but our eyes were lifted again.

As we sang:

> *We are one in the Spirit, we are one in the Lord...*
> *And they'll know we are Christians by our love...*

I remember looking around at my teammates—guys I was sweating beside all summer long—and feeling my heart full.

Not because we had an easy week.
Not because everything went smoothly.
But because our joy had been rekindled.

Not by a moment, but by a *person*—and the Person behind him.

Gordon showed us something we didn't know we were missing. And what he gave us wasn't just a good attitude. It was a picture of what it means to *rejoice in the Lord always*.

REFLECT

Take some time to think through or journal the following:

- How would you describe your current level of joy? What is fueling it—or draining it?
- What do you usually turn to when joy runs low? Does it help long-term?
- What's one thing you can do today to *cultivate joy in the Lord?*

PRAYER

Lord, thank You for being the true source of my joy. I confess that I often base my joy on how things are going, instead of who You are. Help me to rejoice in You always. When I'm tired, be my strength. When I feel empty, fill me with Your presence. Teach me to serve with joy, worship with joy, and lead with joy that overflows into others. In Jesus' name, amen.

HUMILITY

Scripture – Philippians 2:3 (ESV):
"Do nothing from selfish ambition or conceit, but in humility count others more significant than yourselves."

I came into my second summer of camp with confidence. Maybe a little too much of it.

After all, I had a full year of experience under my belt. I knew the rhythm of the schedule, the hidden shortcuts between campfire and the dining hall, the right time to hand out snacks to keep a cabin calm. I'd earned the trust of the directors and had good relationships with returning staff. I had made it through the first-summer gauntlet—and now, I was ready to shine.

In fact, I had convinced myself of something:
This summer, I was going to be the best counselor on staff.

I knew it. I felt it.

And somewhere deep down, I wanted everyone else to know it too.

I didn't say that out loud, of course. But I measured my success each week—how well my campers behaved, how well I delivered devotions, how many times I got recognized for a job well done. I noticed when my name came up in staff meetings. And if I'm being honest, I was already imagining that moment at the end of summer—the staff vote for the "Outstanding Counselor." I could see the applause, the recognition, the satisfaction of being acknowledged.

I thought I had the whole counselor thing figured out.

But then God put Sean on my team.

THE QUIET ONE

Sean didn't stand out at first.

He was quiet, soft-spoken, and preferred to hang back rather than take center stage. He didn't push to lead worship or request the spotlight during skit night. He didn't offer long, eloquent prayers during staff devotions.

But Sean was steady. Solid. Always dependable.

No matter what cabin he was placed in—young campers, older boys, behavioral challenges—he never complained. He didn't roll his eyes at last-minute schedule changes or shift assignments. He just said "yes" and went to work.

He was often the first one to start cleaning and the last one to leave the dining hall. I once found him helping a camper clean up a mess long after everyone else had left for free time. And I never once heard him gripe about the heat, the noise, or the lack of sleep.

He didn't just do his job.
He lived out his calling.
And he did it with *humility*.

At first, I overlooked it. I was too busy trying to prove myself.

But week by week, the contrast between Sean's quiet obedience and my striving heart began to get uncomfortable.

🎯 WHAT IS HUMILITY, REALLY?

Philippians 2:3 hits right at the heart of it:

> *"Do nothing from selfish ambition or conceit, but in humility count others more significant than yourselves."*

Humility isn't self-hatred. It's not insecurity or false modesty.

Humility is having a right view of yourself in light of who God is—and putting others ahead of yourself because that's exactly what Jesus did.

Humility says:

- "I'm not the main character of this story."
- "I'm not here to impress—I'm here to serve."
- "If no one notices me, but someone meets Jesus, that's a win."

I wasn't living that way at the beginning of the summer.

But Sean was.

He never sought recognition. He never looked for praise. But his example began to chip away at my pride.

 ## THE TURNING POINT

Midway through the summer, our staff was exhausted. It had been a hot, demanding week, and everyone was running on fumes.

I remember showing up late to a staff meeting one afternoon. I'd just finished leading a particularly tough group of campers and was internally grumbling about how much I was doing. I sat down frustrated, feeling like no one appreciated how hard I was working.

Then I noticed Sean sitting across the room.

He looked tired too—but he was smiling, listening attentively, encouraging a younger counselor next to him.

No fanfare. No spotlight. Just faithfulness.

I don't know how to describe it exactly, but in that moment, something shifted inside of me. I had been working for recognition. Sean had been working for *Christ*.

I went back to my cabin and prayed, *"God, forgive me. Help me serve like Sean. Help me serve like Jesus."*

A VOTE THAT MATTERED

When the end of summer finally arrived, the directors passed out ballots for the staff to vote on who they believed embodied the mission of the camp—the Outstanding Counselor.

I smiled as I checked a box.
It wasn't mine.

I voted for Sean.
And I told others why they should, too.

Not because he was loud.
Not because he was flashy.
But because he was *faithful*.

He served with humility.
He led with quiet strength.
He lived the Gospel every single day.

HUMILITY CHANGES EVERYTHING

Humility is one of the most underrated traits in Christian leadership. But in God's eyes, it's essential.

It opens the door to **teachability**—you can't grow if you think you already know everything.
It strengthens **teamwork**—when you stop trying to outshine others, you start building something together.
It cultivates **grace**—humble people are quick to forgive, slow to take offense, and more focused on unity than personal victories.

And most importantly, humility reflects Jesus.

Philippians 2 goes on to say that Jesus—though He was *God*—humbled Himself and took on the form of a servant. He washed feet. He touched lepers. He dined with sinners. He gave His life.

And He told us: *"Go and do likewise."*

WHAT DOES HUMILITY LOOK LIKE AT CAMP?

- Letting someone else take the lead when you'd rather be in control
- Volunteering for a tough cabin or cleaning duty without complaining
- Encouraging a teammate even when you feel unseen
- Asking for help when you need it
- Owning your mistakes quickly and honestly
- Choosing what's best for the group—not just what's best for you

You'll be tempted to chase recognition this summer.
You'll be tempted to prove yourself.
But don't fall into that trap.

Choose humility.
It's not flashy. But it's *powerful*.

REFLECT

Take a few quiet moments today and reflect on these questions:

- Why do you think pride sneaks into ministry so easily?
- Can you think of someone on your team who models humility well?
- What's one specific way you can practice humility this week?

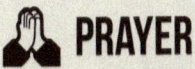

PRAYER

Jesus, thank You for humbling Yourself to serve me. Forgive me for the ways I've made this summer about me—my success, my recognition, my pride. Teach me to count others more significant than myself. Help me lead with humility, love without needing praise, and serve even when no one sees. May I reflect You in the way I walk, speak, and lead. In Your name, amen.

OBEDIENCE

Scripture – John 14:15 (ESV):
"If you love me, you will keep my commandments."

At camp, the weekends feel like gold.

After five packed days of devotions, games, chapels, camper care, lost water bottles, and endless sunscreen reminders, that wave of silence—after the last camper is picked up— is glorious. Staff can finally breathe. You toss your lanyard aside, eat food *not* served on a tray, and maybe even take a full-length shower without a camper banging on the door.

And honestly? That break is needed.

But I also noticed something during my years of summer camp life—something I started to call the "weekend wobble." For some counselors, the weekend wasn't just a time to relax… it was when their faith quietly slipped into cruise control.

They'd "let their hair down"—and sometimes what was underneath wasn't all that godly. 😑

ENTER: TERRY

Terry was a last-minute addition to our staff one summer. You know the type—funny, outgoing, super likable. He bonded with campers quickly, tossed out casual jokes in the dining hall, and always seemed up for a prank or adventure.

During the week, he led devotionals with a chill, relaxed tone. He'd open the Bible, read a few verses, and give a quick 5-minute encouragement like, "Just love God and be good, okay?" Then it was off to archery or the climbing wall.

He wasn't the worst staffer. But he wasn't the most reliable either. He'd skip prep time, be slow to respond when kids needed something, and never really stepped up when extra help was needed. Still, the boys liked him—and that seemed to be enough for him.

But the real disconnect showed up on the weekends.

As soon as the last camper vanished down the gravel road, Terry's "off the clock" self would emerge. He'd grab a couple of guys, head into town, and spend the evening complaining about the camp's "pointless rules" and laughing at the "holier-than-thou" counselors who took things too seriously.

One Saturday, another staffer overheard him at a diner, laughing at an off-color joke and saying, "God doesn't care about this stuff—it's not like it's a sin or anything."

Then Monday would roll around.

Terry would slip back into his role, Bible in hand, ready to deliver another mini-devotional—complete with a reminder that we should "obey God."

I'll be honest—it was jarring.
And it was also convicting.

Not because I was doing the same thing... but because I *knew* how easy it would be to follow that same pattern if I let my guard down.

💬 WHAT OBEDIENCE REALLY MEANS

Jesus doesn't leave much room for confusion in John 14:15: *"If you love me, you will keep my commandments."*

Not "if you love me, post a verse about it."
Not "if you love me, work at a camp."
Not even "if you love me, say the right things."

Jesus ties our *love for Him* directly to our *obedience to Him.*

That's a hard word in a culture where obedience is often seen as oppressive, outdated, or optional. But for a Christian, obedience isn't about rules—it's about *relationship.*

Think of it this way:

- Obedience is a response to love. Not a duty. Not a checklist. It's how we say, "Jesus, I trust You more than I trust myself."

- **Obedience brings protection.** God's commands aren't random—they're guardrails designed to keep us close to Him and safe from harm.

- **Obedience cultivates consistency.** It shapes a life that reflects Christ on *and off* the clock.

🔄 ON AND OFF THE CLOCK

Terry's weekends exposed something important: it's possible to say the right things about God while living like His commands are optional.

But here's the truth: *there is no off-the-clock Christianity.*

When the campers go home, the calling doesn't.
When you're out of uniform, your witness isn't.
When the schedule is flexible, your obedience shouldn't be.

Obedience matters just as much at the diner as it does at the devotion circle.

This doesn't mean we live under constant pressure to be perfect—but it does mean we aim to be *authentic.* Because campers aren't the only ones watching. Your teammates see your life. And more importantly, God does.

✸ WHY OBEDIENCE BRINGS BLESSING

The word "obedience" might feel heavy. Restrictive, even. But in God's kingdom, obedience is the path to freedom.

Here's what obedience brings:

☑ 1. ORDER

Life is chaotic. Camp is loud. Obedience brings divine structure—it centers you on truth and gives clarity to your choices.

◗ 2. PROTECTION

God's commands protect us from the things that wound, enslave, and destroy. They're boundaries, not barriers.

✿ 3. GROWTH

Obedience builds spiritual maturity. It's how roots go deeper. It's how we become trustworthy in leadership.

♡ 4. PEACE

There's peace in knowing you're walking in step with God's will. Your conscience is clear. Your spirit is aligned.

▤ BUILDING A LIFESTYLE OF OBEDIENCE

So how do we *actually* live this out at camp?

📖 STAY IN THE WORD

Start your day in Scripture—even if it's just five minutes. Don't rely on camper devotionals to be your only intake of God's truth.

PRAY FOR STRENGTH

Ask God to help you obey Him—especially when it's hard. Obedience is a work of the Spirit, not just willpower.

 SURROUND YOURSELF WITH ACCOUNTABLE PEOPLE

Spend time with teammates who encourage you toward righteousness, not away from it. Iron sharpens iron.

 BE THE SAME PERSON ON AND OFF DUTY

Don't have two versions of yourself. Be consistent in public and in private. Let your "weekend self" be just as faithful as your "weekday self."

🌀 A LOOK IN THE MIRROR

I've thought a lot about Terry over the years.
I don't think he was a bad guy. I think he was just spiritually unrooted. He knew enough to speak Christian words, but hadn't yet surrendered to Christian living.

Camp isn't just a place to serve—it's a place to grow. And obedience is one of the clearest markers of that growth.

So let me ask you:

- Are you obeying out of love?
- Are you walking the walk—or just talking the talk?
- Are you the same person when no one's watching?

If you're not sure—go to Jesus. He's not asking for perfection. He's asking for *your heart.*

And when He has it, obedience becomes a joy—not a burden.

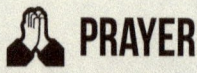 REFLECT

Take a few moments today and reflect or journal on these:

- In what areas of your life is it hardest to obey God right now?
- Are there places in your camp routine where your actions and words don't match?
- What changes can you make this week to live more consistently with the truth you teach?

PRAYER

Jesus, thank You for loving me first. Help me love You not just with my words, but with my life. Teach me to obey You—even when it's not easy, even when no one is looking. Guard my heart from hypocrisy, and shape my life into one that honors You in every setting. I want to follow You with all I am. Help me walk in obedience, rooted in love. In Your name, amen.

COMPASSION

Scripture – Colossians 3:12 (ESV):
"Put on then, as God's chosen ones, holy and beloved, compassionate hearts, kindness, humility, meekness, and patience."

There are campers you never forget—for better or for worse.

Most of my summers were filled with cabin groups full of hilarious, energetic, respectful kids. They followed the schedule, cracked jokes, engaged in devotions, and made those long weeks feel like a gift.

But every now and then... there's a camper who tests every ounce of patience you have. The one who stretches you to your limit. The one who leaves you whispering prayers like, *"Lord, why me?"*

For me, that camper was Jaime.

THE BUTTON-PUSHER

That summer, my home church had sent a group of boys to attend camp. My dad, always with a heart for kids who needed a break from their chaotic lives, had sponsored three brothers from a particularly rough background. These boys had lived through more hurt than most kids ever should.

I was assigned Jaime—the middle brother.

He wasn't just challenging. He was *next level*.

Jaime was loud, defiant, and completely uninterested in the camp experience. While the other campers bonded and laughed their way through rec time and devotions, Jaime pushed every button I had.

He showed up late to nearly every activity.
He refused to shower.
He complained—loudly—about the food.
He argued constantly, especially with campers who didn't look like him.
And one morning, before breakfast, he straight-up *ran away* from camp... to find cigarettes.

That little field trip ended with a visit from the local sheriff's department.

Compassion? I had none left.

I was embarrassed. Frustrated. Worn out. And honestly, I just wanted him to go home.

But God wasn't finished with Jaime.
And He wasn't finished with *me*, either.

WHEN SOMEONE ELSE SEES WHAT YOU CAN'T

Another counselor in my unit named Eric noticed how hard Jaime was making my week. He wasn't assigned to Jaime's cabin. He didn't have to deal with the daily stress. But Eric saw the situation—and more importantly, he saw the *person*.

Eric started showing up at meals and gently engaging Jaime in conversation. He offered to walk with him to activities when I was about ready to drag him there. He even took time during his free hour to play basketball with Jaime, one-on-one. No lectures. No forced messages. Just presence.

And something started to shift.

Jaime's walls didn't fall all at once. But by the final night of camp, he was more respectful. He stayed close to the group. He even sang along quietly during worship.

Eric's compassion did what my frustration never could—it softened his heart.

 ## THE REALITY OF HARD CAMPERS

Let's not sugarcoat it—some campers are difficult.
They come with trauma, defenses, and learned behavior from rough lives. They don't always know how to accept kindness. Some fight against authority, against structure, against *you*.

But behind every outburst... behind every smart-aleck comment or act of defiance... is a kid who *desperately needs Jesus.*

And more than your perfectly prepared devotions or detailed schedule, they need to feel **seen**, **valued**, and **loved**.

Colossians 3:12 reminds us to *"put on... compassionate hearts, kindness, humility, meekness, and patience."*

Did you catch that?

We're told to *put on* compassion. That means it's not always natural. It doesn't just appear when we wake up. It's a choice—a layer of Christlike character we have to wear with intention.

Compassion is **proactive**.
It steps in when frustration wants to walk out.
It serves when comfort wants to sit down.
It loves even when love hasn't been earned.

THE LONG-TERM IMPACT

Many years passed after that summer, and honestly, I had mostly moved on from the Jaime saga.

Then one day, I ran into him—older now, a man grown.
He recognized me first.

We talked for a bit, catching up on life. And then he said something that stopped me in my tracks:

"You and Eric showed me something that week. I didn't know what to call it at the time, but I knew it was different. You didn't give up on me. And that stuck with me. I still can't shake the feeling that maybe Jesus is real—and maybe He actually changes people."

I don't know where Jaime is now in his faith journey. I don't know the full outcome. But I do know this:

Compassion planted something in him that week.
Not a sermon. Not a rulebook. Not a punishment.
Compassion.

WHY CAMPERS NEED MORE THAN RULES

Camp life runs on structure. Schedules. Boundaries. And those are all good things. But structure alone doesn't change hearts.

Rules may correct behavior, but compassion opens the door to transformation.

Here's what I've learned:

- Compassion sees beyond the behavior to the pain behind it.
- Compassion listens first instead of jumping to judgment.
- Compassion shows up again and again—even when it's not appreciated right away.

It doesn't excuse sin. It doesn't ignore boundaries. But it reflects the heart of Jesus, who *ate with outcasts, touched the untouchables, and wept with the hurting.*

 ## WHEN YOU FEEL LIKE YOU HAVE NOTHING LEFT

You're going to have a Jaime. Maybe more than one.

And there will be moments when compassion feels impossible. You'll feel tired. Angry. Ready to throw your hands in the air.

When that happens, remember this:

Compassion isn't something you produce on your own—it's something God pours through you.

Go to Him.
Ask Him to soften your heart.
Ask Him to help you see that difficult camper the way *He* sees them.

Then take a breath... and stay.

Sometimes the most Christlike thing you can do is simply *not give up.*

HOW TO GROW A COMPASSIONATE HEART

Here are a few ways to cultivate compassion in the chaos of camp life:

1. PRAY FOR YOUR CAMPERS BY NAME

Especially the ones you're struggling with. It's hard to stay bitter toward someone you're consistently lifting up to Jesus.

2. LEARN THEIR STORY

Ask gentle questions. Look past the behavior. Every camper has a backstory that helps explain why they act the way they do.

3. SERVE IN SMALL WAYS

A kind word. A helping hand. A patient tone. Small acts of compassion build trust and break down walls.

4. STAY SPIRITUALLY ROOTED

Spend time in God's presence. You can't give what you don't have. Let Him fill you so you can pour out.

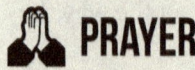

REFLECT

Pause and reflect or journal your thoughts:

- Who is your "Jaime" right now? How are you responding to them?
- Have you ever seen compassion change someone's heart?
- What's one step you can take today to extend compassion when it's hard?

PRAYER

Lord, thank You for showing me compassion when I least deserved it. Teach me to love like You do—to see beyond behavior and meet people in their brokenness. When I grow weary, give me strength. When I want to walk away, help me stay. Fill me with Your heart so I can reflect Your kindness to every camper You've entrusted to me. In Jesus' name, amen

ENDURANCE

Scripture – Hebrews 12:1 (ESV):
"Therefore, since we are surrounded by so great a cloud of witnesses, let us also lay aside every weight, and sin which clings so closely, and let us run with endurance the race that is set before us."

There's tired... and then there's *last-week-of-camp tired*.

It's the kind of tired that seeps into your bones. The kind where your legs ache, your eyes burn, and your brain can't string three thoughts together without needing caffeine or a nap—or both.

That's where I was in early August one summer. I had been at camp since the *end of May*. Every week had been full—physically, emotionally, spiritually. And while camp had brought incredible moments of joy and connection, it had also brought the kind of weariness you don't fully understand until you've lived it.

The final week had arrived. I was exhausted. And like most of the returning staff, I was hoping for one thing: **clean-up crew.**

THE COVETED ASSIGNMENT

See, the last week of camp had lower attendance. To wrap things up, the directors would divide the staff in two. Half would continue cabin duties, while the other half would be assigned to the "clean-up crew"—a kind of end-of-summer maintenance squad helping prep camp for the off-season.

Now normally, "clean-up duty" doesn't sound like a reward. But to us? It was golden. A break from the daily grind of small groups, late-night devos, and high-energy games. It meant quieter days, simple tasks, and—if we were lucky—some free time.

Secretly (okay, not so secretly), **everyone** wanted clean-up crew.

But when assignments came out, I wasn't just left off the list—I was sent to a completely *different* cabin unit. With **younger boys.** You know, the ones who require more supervision, more reminders, more "please don't lick that" conversations.

I was frustrated. Tired. Disappointed. Honestly? I was *mad*.

I had given everything I had all summer long. Couldn't I coast just a little bit for the final week?

A NEW CABIN, A NEW CHALLENGE

I stepped into my new assignment with a forced smile and a weary heart. The campers were younger than I was used to, and the first couple of days felt more like babysitting than leading.

There was one boy in particular who nearly broke me.

During our unit's special night hike—an under-the-stars campout that usually brought awe and bonding—this kid *whined* from the first step.

"It's too far."
"My feet hurt."
"There are bugs."
"Why do we even have to do this?"

Halfway through the trail, he simply stopped walking altogether. Sat down in the dirt. Arms crossed. Refused to move.

And so... I carried him.

On my back.
The entire rest of the trail.

Not exactly the peaceful final-week memory I had envisioned.

But somewhere in the middle of all that frustration, another camper named Ethan caught my eye.

✦ ETHAN'S WEEK

Ethan was curious. Kind. He had a sincere interest in everything we did—from devotionals to archery to singing by the fire. There was a light in him that made me want to keep going, even when I had nothing left in the tank.

So I poured into him.

I asked questions during meals. I shared stories of God's faithfulness during devotions. I prayed for him each night before lights out. I gave it everything I had left.

I was tired. But something told me Ethan needed my best.

By the end of the week, I wasn't just dragging my feet to the finish line—I was finishing with joy.

Little did I know, the *real* finish line was still ahead.

🏠 A DIVINE SURPRISE

A few weeks later, I visited a local church near my college campus. The moment I walked through the doors, I saw a familiar face—Ethan.

He saw me too. His eyes lit up. He waved excitedly and pointed me out to his mom. It was a sweet moment.

Then, at the end of the service, the pastor made an announcement:
"Today, a young man in our church family has decided to commit his life to Jesus."

It was Ethan.

My heart could've burst.

After the service, Ethan's mom found me. With tears in her eyes, she said,
"When Ethan saw you walk in, he told me right away—'That's my camp counselor. That's how I know today is the day.'"

He took my presence that day as confirmation. God had been working in his heart all along, but that *moment*—that divine, unexpected moment—became the spark of surrender.

And all I could think was: *What if I had mailed it in that week? What if I had walked through that cabin half-heartedly, just trying to survive?*

RUNNING WITH ENDURANCE

Hebrews 12:1 challenges us:
"Let us run with endurance the race that is set before us."

Not sprint. Not jog when it's easy. Not walk when we feel like it.
Run. With endurance.

And not just any race—**the race set before us.**
The one God *chose* for us.
Even when we're tired. Even when we'd rather be somewhere else. Even when we're carrying campers—literally or figuratively—on our backs.

That's when it counts the most.

YOU'RE NOT RUNNING ALONE

Here's what gives me hope when I hit the wall:

- **Endurance isn't about willpower—it's about perspective.** When I fix my eyes on Jesus instead of my exhaustion, something shifts.
- **Endurance isn't about impressing—it's about faithfulness.** God isn't asking for perfection. He's asking for perseverance.
- **Endurance isn't done alone.** We're surrounded by a "great cloud of witnesses"—those who've gone before us and the ones running beside us now.

Jesus is with you in every step. He sees your weariness. He understands it. And He promises to be your strength when yours runs out.

 # HOW TO ENDURE WHEN YOU'RE EMPTY

Here are a few ways to stay the course when camp feels like it's too much:

REFOCUS DAILY

Start your day with God, even when it's tempting to hit snooze. Even five minutes of Scripture and prayer can reset your heart.

🌢 REST WHEN YOU CAN

True endurance includes wise rest. Drink water. Take deep breaths. Nap during your break if you can. God honors stewardship of your body.

💬 ASK FOR ENCOURAGEMENT

Tell a teammate you're struggling. Let them lift you up in prayer. Sometimes the race feels lighter when we run it together.

🎯 REMEMBER WHY YOU STARTED

Think back to what brought you here. Remember the calling. Remember the impact. Your "yes" still matters.

 **REFLECT**

Take a moment to pause and ask:

- Where am I feeling worn down right now?
- Who is my "Ethan"? Is there someone who needs my full attention and energy—right now?
- What would it look like to finish strong—not in my strength, but with my eyes fixed on Jesus?

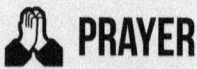 **PRAYER**

Jesus, I am tired. You know how long this race has felt. But I don't want to give up. Teach me to run with endurance, not in my own strength, but in Yours. Help me keep going—not just to survive camp, but to finish well. Use even my weakest moments to reveal Your power. I trust that You are working in ways I can't yet see. In Your name, amen.

INTEGRITY

Scripture – Proverbs 10:9 (ESV):
"Whoever walks in integrity walks securely, but he who makes his ways crooked will be found out."

═══════════════════════════

Some lessons in leadership are learned by watching someone do it *right*.
Others? You learn by watching when it all falls apart.

This is one of those stories.

It was supposed to be one of the best summers our family had ever experienced. My oldest daughter, a rising senior in college, had been hired in the spring to help lead camp-wide programming. She was creative, organized, spiritually grounded, and eager to make the summer special. It was a role tailor-made for her gifts.

My son, who had just graduated high school that June, was hired as an assistant counselor. It would be his first big step into young adult leadership, and the fact that he and his sister would be at camp together felt like a gift from God.

As a dad—and as someone who had devoted years of my life to Christian camps—I was thrilled. I imagined the stories they'd come home with, the friendships they'd form, and the impact they'd have on campers.

But what started with so much promise... ended with deep disappointment.

A HOUSE WITHOUT A FOUNDATION

It didn't fall apart all at once.

At first, it was small things—programming plans made in staff meetings that were suddenly reversed without explanation. Promises made by the camp director, only to be broken a few days later. Expectations constantly shifting. Conversations happening behind closed doors, but never followed up with clarity.

The programming team that was supposed to support my daughter often disappeared—avoiding responsibility, making excuses, and even lying to avoid confrontation. When mistakes were made, no one owned them. When issues were raised, they were ignored or swept aside.

And my son—just trying to do his job and grow as a young leader—watched as adults around him played favorites, blamed others, and operated with double standards.

It wasn't one bad day or one poor decision. It was the slow erosion of trust through a hundred tiny compromises.

By mid-summer, team unity was gone. Motivation had dried up. The staff wasn't just discouraged—they were disillusioned.

⚠️ THE FALLOUT

The worst part wasn't the mistakes. Every leader makes them.
The worst part was the lack of integrity.

When people lie to cover their failures...
When leaders say one thing but live another...
When silence replaces accountability...
When truth is replaced with spin...

The damage goes deep.

That summer ended with a group of young adults—many of them future ministry leaders—walking away not inspired, but wounded. My children included.

And the fallout didn't end with the closing day of camp.

The leadership was released from their roles that off-season due to the growing number of complaints. But the impact lingered. The camp struggled for years to rebuild staff trust and camper enrollment. The reputation that had taken decades to build was shaken in a matter of weeks.

Why?

Because integrity is the foundation of everything.
And once it cracks... the whole structure is in danger.

INTEGRITY IS WHO YOU ARE WHEN NO ONE'S LOOKING

Proverbs 10:9 is clear:
"Whoever walks in integrity walks securely, but he who makes his ways crooked will be found out."

Let's break that down:

- **Integrity brings security.** It creates trust. It gives peace. It allows you to lead boldly and live freely because you have nothing to hide.
- **Crooked paths catch up with you.** You might get away with it for a while—but eventually, the truth surfaces. And when it does, trust is gone.

Integrity isn't about being perfect. It's about being *consistent*—the same person in public and in private, on the platform and behind the scenes.

It's choosing what's right over what's easy.
It's being honest even when it costs you something.
It's following through when no one's checking.
It's apologizing when you've messed up.
It's leading from conviction, not convenience.

At camp, that means your integrity is tested *every single day*—in small choices and quiet moments.

WHAT INTEGRITY LOOKS LIKE AT CAMP

Here's what walking in integrity might look like in your current role:

- You prep your devotions even when no one will know how much time you spent.
- You clean up after your cabin even if someone else made the mess.
- You speak truth in meetings—even when it's uncomfortable.
- You admit when you're wrong—without blaming others.
- You don't stretch the truth just to make a better story.
- You treat each camper with kindness—even if they're difficult or different.

It's not flashy. It won't always be praised.
But it's what builds trust—and what multiplies your influence.

 ## INTEGRITY HAS A RIPPLE EFFECT

The most heartbreaking part of that summer wasn't that things got messy. It was that so many *good* young leaders walked away with a damaged view of Christian leadership.

It reminded me that your example doesn't just affect your week—it can affect someone's entire perception of faith.

That's a heavy truth. But it's also an *opportunity*.

When you choose integrity—especially when others don't—you're showing the world what Jesus is really like. You're reminding your team, your campers, and your camp that there *is* a better way.

And believe me: they'll remember.

🔦 INTEGRITY STARTS IN THE SHADOWS

Most people won't see your quiet choices.
They won't know about the camper you prayed over late at night.
They won't hear the words you didn't say during a tense conversation.
They won't notice the shortcut you refused to take.

But God sees.
And He honors it.

Integrity is forged in the shadows.
And one day, it will shine in the light.

REFLECT

Spend a few minutes thinking or journaling through these questions:

- In what areas of your camp life are you most tempted to compromise?
- Have you ever seen integrity change the direction of a situation—or the opposite?
- What's one small act of integrity you can commit to this week?

PRAYER

God, help me walk in integrity. I don't want to just say the right things—I want to live them. Search my heart. Show me where I've been cutting corners or hiding behind excuses. Give me courage to be consistent in every area of my life, even when no one's watching. May the way I live reflect You clearly and bring trust, peace, and healing to those around me. In Jesus' name, amen.

PRAYER

Scripture – 1 Thessalonians 5:17 (ESV):
"pray without ceasing."

Prayer isn't a box to check.
It's not just a spiritual warm-up before meals.
It's not the thing we do when we've run out of other options.

Prayer is the breath of the Christian life.
It's the ongoing, honest, life-giving connection between you and your Creator.
And if there's one thing I've learned after decades of camp leadership and youth ministry—it's this:

When prayer saturates the camp, lives change. Period.

A CULTURE OF PRAYER

As an adult, I've had the opportunity to serve in a variety of roles—church camps, youth mission trips, leadership retreats. Different camps. Different leaders. Different styles. But the one thing the strongest teams always had in common?

Prayer.

I've seen leaders who understood that their strength, insight, and planning would only get them so far. They knew the real battle was spiritual—and it had to be fought on their knees.

One church camp had a beautiful system in place: they handed out "prayer bracelets" to church members before camp even began. Each bracelet had the name of a camper. People wore them as a daily reminder to intercede for that student. I watched teenagers who had no idea someone was praying for them encounter Jesus in life-altering ways. Coincidence? Not a chance.

That same church opened its sanctuary during camp week. Anyone—parents, church members, even grandparents—could walk in during the day, sit quietly, and pray over the names of campers and staff. And they did. Every day. Dozens of voices lifting up the same request: *"God, move in power."*

Meanwhile, back at camp, we weren't leaving prayer to chance either. We scheduled it into the rhythm of our day. Counselors met in small groups to pray over one another before the campers even stirred in the morning. At night, you could find clusters of staff sitting in hammocks or by cabin steps, whispering prayers for the kids they were shepherding.

And then there were the quiet moments—the ones no one else saw. I've watched counselors sit at the edge of their beds, hands folded, eyes closed, lifting up names they'd just met 48 hours before.

It wasn't flashy. But it was powerful.

THE EVIDENCE IS EVERYWHERE

Over the years, I've seen too many lives changed to chalk it up to good programming. I've watched chains of addiction fall off. I've seen hardened hearts softened. I've witnessed reconciliation between broken families, confession between friends, repentance at altars, and joy fill the face of someone who had only known despair.

In every setting, at every camp, in every mission trip I've been a part of, there's been one undeniable force at work: prayer.

Not the kind of prayer that's rushed through before a meal or spoken from a stage just to start a meeting.

But the kind of prayer that *wrestles*. That *waits*. That *believes*.

WHAT DOES "PRAY WITHOUT CEASING" REALLY MEAN?

1 Thessalonians 5:17 says it plainly: *"pray without ceasing."*

At first glance, that might seem impossible. We can't all walk around with our eyes closed and heads bowed all day long, right?

But Paul wasn't talking about posture. He was talking about presence.

To "pray without ceasing" is to live your entire life in *awareness of God's nearness*. It's about staying connected—not just occasionally, but constantly. Like keeping a conversation going with someone who's always beside you. Whispered prayers. Quick thank-yous. Honest cries for help. Silent moments of surrender.

Here's what that kind of prayer looks like at camp:

- Praying before you open your mouth in morning devotions.
- Whispering, *"Help me, Lord,"* before confronting a conflict.
- Thanking God as you watch a camper take a next step in faith.
- Asking for patience under your breath before responding to a difficult camper.
- Inviting God to lead your thoughts during a walk to the dining hall.

Prayer isn't always loud. But it's always *available*.

WHEN YOU DON'T FEEL LIKE PRAYING

Let's be real—there will be days you don't feel like praying. Days when you're tired. Discouraged. Maybe even spiritually dry.

Those are the days you need it the most.

Prayer is not a reward for spiritual strength—it's a source of it.

When you feel weak, pray.
When you feel empty, pray.
When you don't have the words, pray anyway.

Romans 8:26 reminds us that even when we don't know what to pray, the Spirit intercedes for us with groanings too deep for words. You are never alone in your prayers.

CREATING A RHYTHM OF PRAYER

If you want to build your life on prayer, you don't need to start with an hour. You just need to start.

Here are a few simple practices that can help:

📖 1. MORNING ANCHORS

Begin your day with five minutes in prayer—before you check your phone, before you talk to anyone else. Offer God your day. Ask Him to lead you.

⏸ 2. MIDDAY CHECK-INS

Take 30 seconds between rotations, during snack time, or while walking between activities. Breathe. Acknowledge God. Reconnect.

🧍 3. WALK AND PRAY

Instead of using all your free time to scroll or nap, take a walk and pray. Talk to God about your campers, your team, your heart.

🙌 4. PRAY WITH OTHERS

Don't be afraid to grab a teammate and say, "Can we pray about this real quick?" Let prayer be a natural part of your community.

🌙 5. END-OF-DAY REFLECTION

Before you close your eyes at night, thank God for specific moments. Confess any failures. Ask Him to redeem tomorrow.

✦ CAMP RUNS ON PRAYER

Camp doesn't run on coffee and bug spray—it runs on prayer.

If you want to see God move, you must invite Him to move.
If you want campers to experience transformation, you must intercede.
If you want your own heart to stay soft, your own strength to stay renewed, your own spirit to stay centered—pray.

Because every breakthrough starts with a prayer.
Every life changed began with someone whispering, *"God, please work."*

REFLECT

Pause and take a few minutes to reflect or journal:

- What does your current prayer life look like at camp? Is it consistent or casual?
- Have you seen the power of prayer at work in your life or others this summer?
- What would it look like for you to "pray without ceasing" in your daily rhythm?

PRAYER

Father, remind me that prayer is not a duty, but a gift. Help me to stay connected to You throughout each day—not just in set moments, but in every conversation, every challenge, every step. Teach me to rely on You, to listen for You, to cry out to You, and to thank You. Fill me with faith that You are working even when I can't see it. I give You this day—lead me, shape me, and speak to me. In Jesus' name, amen.

FAITH

Scripture – Hebrews 11:1 (ESV):
"Now faith is the assurance of things hoped for, the conviction of things not seen."

═══════════════════════════

Nobody really knows what they're signing up for when they say "yes" to working at summer camp.

Sure, there are job descriptions, planning meetings, packing lists, and plenty of pep talks. But no amount of preparation can fully predict the *impact* camp will have on you.

Most counselors come with hope in their hearts—that it'll be a fun summer, that they'll make new friends, that God might even do something meaningful in a camper's life. But what many don't expect is how deeply *they themselves* will be changed.

And it all begins with one simple thing: **faith.**

Faith to step into something unfamiliar.

Faith to believe your "yes" matters.
Faith to trust that God can do more in eight weeks than you ever imagined.

THE HIDDEN IMPACT

If there's one truth I've seen again and again in camp ministry, it's this:

God is using camp to raise up the next generation of spiritual leaders.

So many pastors, missionaries, youth workers, and church leaders trace their calling back to a summer at camp. Not because they had some huge spotlight moment, but because they had space to listen. To serve. To struggle. To grow.

And it didn't happen all at once.
It happened through **faithfulness**.

It happened in the early mornings before the campers woke up.
It happened during devotionals, when the Spirit stirred something deeper.
It happened in the messes—when the schedule broke down, when the plan failed, when a camper's question had no easy answer.
And it happened in the quiet moments when someone said, *"God, I don't know what I'm doing—but I trust You."*

That's **faith**.

WHAT FAITH ACTUALLY LOOKS LIKE

Hebrews 11:1 gives us a beautiful definition:
"Now faith is the assurance of things hoped for, the conviction of things not seen."

Faith isn't just belief—it's **confidence** in what hasn't happened yet.
It's **conviction** that even though you can't see the full story, you know the Author.
It's choosing to walk forward even when the next step is foggy.

And around camp, that kind of faith shows up in all kinds of ways:

- **Trusting God's promises** when circumstances seem bleak or discouraging.
- **Stepping out to lead** even when you don't feel qualified.
- **Believing God can change a camper's heart**, even when you've seen no progress.
- **Opening up about your struggles** with your team, trusting that vulnerability builds community.
- **Holding onto what's true in Scripture**, even when emotions tell a different story.
- **Waiting on God** when the breakthrough doesn't come on your timetable.

Faith isn't just for the mountaintop moments—it's for *every moment*.

YOU DON'T HAVE TO SEE THE FULL PICTURE

One of the hardest things about faith is learning to live in the tension of "not yet."

You won't always see the fruit of your efforts right away.
You won't always know how God is using your words, your presence, or your prayers.
You may not get the recognition or the resolution you hoped for.

But that's exactly where faith thrives.

Because faith doesn't require you to have all the answers. It only requires that you trust the One who *does*.

And when you can't see the road ahead, faith anchors you in what you *do* know:

- God is good.
- God is present.
- God is working.

Always.

 ## REAL FAITH LEAVES A LEGACY

I've seen it firsthand. Young counselors, full of passion but unsure of their path, step into camp by faith—and leave forever changed.

They came to serve for a summer, but God was planting something eternal.

Some returned to college with a renewed sense of purpose.
Some felt called into ministry or missions.
Some started leading small groups or mentoring others.
Some simply went home with a deeper walk with Jesus and a burning desire to make Him known.

But none of that happened because they had a perfect plan. It happened because they said, *"Yes, Lord. I trust You."*

WALKING BY FAITH, NOT BY SIGHT

Faith doesn't remove difficulty—it just reframes it.

You'll still have hard days. You'll still face setbacks. You'll still wonder if you're making a difference. But faith says, *"I don't need to see the whole picture—I just need to trust the One holding the brush."*

You may be exhausted.
You may be uncertain.
You may be feeling invisible.

But you are *not* unseen.
You are *not* forgotten.
And you are *not* wasting your time.

God sees your quiet obedience.
God hears your whispered prayers.
God honors your faith.

HOW TO BUILD YOUR FAITH AT CAMP

If you want to grow in faith this summer, don't wait for a crisis. Start small. Start steady. Start now.

1. REMEMBER GOD'S FAITHFULNESS

Write down ways you've seen God move in your life. Look back often. What He's done before, He can do again.

2. SEEK TRUTH IN SCRIPTURE

Read His Word daily. Let truth ground you when emotions shift and circumstances wobble.

3. SURROUND YOURSELF WITH FAITH-FILLED PEOPLE

Lean on your team. Share your doubts. Let others lift your eyes when your vision gets cloudy.

4. CONFESS UNBELIEF HONESTLY

God's not scared of your questions. Tell Him when you're struggling. Ask Him to help your unbelief (Mark 9:24).

5. PRACTICE GRATITUDE

Faith and gratitude go hand in hand. When you thank God for what you have, your heart becomes more expectant for what He'll do.

6. WAIT WELL

Faith doesn't rush. Trust God's timing. Some seeds take time to grow.

🌱 REFLECT

Take a few moments today to reflect or journal on these questions:

- In what areas of camp life are you being asked to walk by faith right now?
- What are you trusting God for this summer—even if you haven't seen the results yet?
- How has your faith grown since the beginning of this camp season?

 PRAYER

Lord, I want to trust You more. I confess that sometimes I want answers more than I want You. But I believe You're working, even when I can't see it. Help me walk by faith, not by sight. Give me confidence in Your promises, courage when I feel uncertain, and endurance when I grow tired. Thank You for calling me to this place. I trust that my "yes" matters. In Jesus' name, amen.

SELFLESSNESS

Scripture – Romans 12:10 (ESV):
"Love one another with brotherly affection.
Outdo one another in showing honor."

Every summer, there's at least one staffer who just *gets it*.

They don't need a bunch of reminders. They're not in it for the praise or the Instagram post. From day one, they come ready to serve—with joy, humility, and zero need to be noticed.

They're the ones who see the extra need and fill it before being asked. They notice the counselor who looks discouraged and speak life into them. They do the quiet, behind-the-scenes things that no one else volunteers for.

For me, one of those people was Brock.

THE COUNSELOR WHO NEVER NEEDED CREDIT

I worked with Brock during a summer where the days were long, the schedule was tight, and rest was rare. Like most camps, staff breaks were short—and sacred. That hour or two each day was your chance to exhale. To breathe. To be human again.

So when another counselor overslept and didn't return from his break on time, it caused frustration. The cabin was left unsupervised, the schedule backed up, and people were annoyed.

But Brock? He didn't complain.

He gave up his *own* break to cover. Quietly. Without fuss. Without pointing fingers. He just stepped in and said, *"I've got it."*

That's who he was.

He was always looking for ways to love people *well*. Always taking the low place. Always quick to honor others, and quick to submit to the leadership with a servant's heart. Whether it was cleaning up a mess he didn't make, helping set up before chapel, or praying with someone who was struggling, Brock just *showed up*—with no desire for recognition, just a heart to reflect Jesus.

And the thing is... people noticed. Not because he talked about it, but because **his life preached it.**

🫶 THE GOSPEL CALLS US TO LAY OURSELVES DOWN

Romans 12:10 gives us one of the clearest calls in Scripture for how we're to live in community:

"Love one another with brotherly affection. Outdo one another in showing honor."

The Gospel isn't just about being saved from something—it's about being transformed *for* something.

Jesus laid His life down for us. Now He calls us to lay our lives down for each other.

That means camp isn't just about campers. It's about how we treat our **fellow staff.** The way you speak to, serve, and sacrifice for the people on your team is *just as important* as how you serve your cabin.

And in a high-stress, non-stop environment like camp, selflessness doesn't happen naturally. It has to be **chosen.**

✋ SELFLESSNESS VS. SELF-PRESERVATION

It's easy to start the summer with a servant's heart. But as the weeks go on, fatigue sets in. Frustration bubbles up. You start keeping score:

- "I took out the trash last time."
- "Why do I always have to be the one to step in?"
- "No one notices the extra things I do."

And before long, the mission shifts from *serve others* to *protect myself.*

Let's be real: the temptation to self-preserve is real. But the Gospel calls us to something *better.*

Selflessness isn't about being a doormat. It's about *choosing* to lay down your preferences so someone else can thrive.

It's not weakness. It's strength under control.

⚡ THE POWER OF OUTDOING EACH OTHER IN HONOR

I love how Paul doesn't just say "show honor"—he says *outdo* one another in showing honor.

It's like a **holy competition:**
You want to be the first to serve. The first to encourage. The first to offer help. Not because you're trying to earn anything, but because love compels you.

When a staff team lives this way, it changes everything.

There's no room for bitterness—because honor leads.
There's no need for comparison—because everyone's lifting each other up.
There's no space for pride—because everyone's racing to get *lower.*

That's what Brock modeled.
And that's what we're all called to become.

✦ WHAT SELFLESSNESS LOOKS LIKE AT CAMP

It's not always dramatic. Often, it's *ordinary* moments filled with eternal meaning.

- Giving up your break so a teammate can rest.
- Letting someone else lead when you wanted the spotlight.
- Cleaning the cabin without being asked.
- Choosing to listen instead of argue.
- Running toward the problem when others step back.
- Praying for the person who frustrates you.

And perhaps the hardest one:

- Trusting leadership even when you don't agree—and choosing to support rather than complain.

Brock did that. Over and over. His selflessness wasn't loud—but it left a lasting impact.

🕊 WHY SELFLESSNESS IS SO RARE—AND SO NEEDED

We live in a "me first" world. A world that tells us to chase recognition, protect our time, and seek comfort.

But Jesus says, *"If anyone would come after me, let him deny himself and take up his cross daily and follow me"* (Luke 9:23).

Camp gives us the perfect training ground for that kind of life. Every day you wake up, you get a new chance to say: *"Not my will, Lord—but Yours. Not my preferences, but what's best for my team. Not my comfort, but someone else's need."*

That's selflessness.
And it's *beautiful*.

💭 YOU WON'T REGRET LAYING YOUR LIFE DOWN

I've never met a counselor who regretted sacrificing their own comfort to serve others. But I *have* seen many regret the moments they missed because they were too focused on themselves.

You have no idea what your small acts of selflessness might unlock.

That one break you give up?
It might help a teammate hold it together.

That one encouraging word?
It might be the reason someone doesn't quit.

That one prayer you pray?
It might be the spark that leads a camper to Jesus.

You don't have to be Brock. You just have to be *willing*.

 **REFLECT**

Take a few moments today to reflect or journal on these:

- Are there places this summer where you've been tempted to self-protect instead of serve?
- Who on your team can you honor this week— not because they earned it, but because you love them?
- What's one tangible way you can practice selflessness today?

 **PRAYER**

Jesus, thank You for laying down everything for me. Teach me to love like You do—to live with open hands and an open heart. Help me see the needs of others and choose to serve, even when it's hard. Guard my heart from pride and comparison. Help me to outdo my teammates in showing honor and build a camp culture of selfless love. Use my life—every break, every quiet act, every choice—to reflect You. In Your name, amen.

COURAGE

Scripture – Joshua 1:9 (ESV):
"Have I not commanded you? Be strong and courageous. Do not be frightened, and do not be dismayed, for the Lord your God is with you wherever you go."

Let's be honest: some people are just wired for camp.

They love the dirt-under-the-fingernails lifestyle. They're energized by games, hikes, late-night conversations, loud worship, and quiet early-morning devotionals with coffee and bug spray. They bring duct tape, granola bars, and spare flashlights like they're heading into the wilderness for a month—and they're *thrilled about it.*

My wife? Was *not* one of those people.

She's talented. Called. Wise. Deeply devoted to Christ.

But "outdoorsy"? Not even close.

Let's just say a two-star hotel feels like roughing it to her.

So when God called her to spend a summer as a *Christian camp counselor*—with no air conditioning, no guaranteed hot showers, and plenty of bugs—it didn't just take a willing heart.

It took **courage**.

OUT OF HER COMFORT ZONE

During her college years, my wife served every summer on traveling praise and worship teams, singing at three to five churches per week. It was her lane, her passion, and the kind of ministry that made sense for her gifts.

But following her sophomore year, vocal issues began to surface. Her voice needed rest. Touring was no longer an option. And that left her in an unexpected place—open, uncertain, and listening for a new calling.

That's when she heard about a girls-only Christian camp that was in desperate need of counselors. The moment she read the description, she knew: this was *not* her dream gig.

No air conditioning. Hiking. Bugs. Sleeping in cabins with a dozen middle school girls. Worship with an acoustic guitar instead of a sound system. And worst of all (in her mind at the time): *campfire smoke in her hair.*

But there was a tug in her heart. A whisper: *"Go."*

So she did.

And it changed her life.

COURAGE LOOKS DIFFERENT FOR EVERYONE

We often think of courage as something loud and dramatic—standing up to injustice, rescuing someone from danger, preaching to a stadium full of people.

But sometimes courage looks like saying "yes" to something that *terrifies* you.

Sometimes courage means stepping into the unknown.
Sometimes it means showing up when you feel unqualified.
Sometimes it means trusting God when you'd rather stay safe.
Sometimes it means relying on others, asking for help, and letting go of control.

For my wife, it meant trusting God through a week of sweat, mosquitoes, and stretching conversations. It meant bonding with girls over late-night prayers and learning that God could use her *even without her voice*. It meant watching God use her faithfulness to plant seeds in young hearts that would bear fruit for *years* to come.

COURAGE BUILDS CALLINGS

That summer sparked something deep in her—a renewed sense of God's call to use her musical gifts for youth ministry.

After camp, she returned home not only with new friendships and a fresh perspective, but a burning desire to lead worship in a way that discipled the next generation.

That calling eventually blossomed into a *worship ministry* that impacted scores of girls for almost two decades. Many of them are now leading worship across the country and around the world—all because one college girl had the courage to say *yes* to something unfamiliar.

That's the thing about courage:
It doesn't just change your summer. It can change your *story*.

 ## GOD'S PRESENCE IS THE SOURCE OF OUR COURAGE

In Joshua 1:9, God tells Joshua—who is about to lead Israel into the Promised Land—*"Be strong and courageous. Do not be frightened, and do not be dismayed, for the Lord your God is with you wherever you go."*

The command is bold, but the reason is even better:
God is with you.

You're not called to courage because *you're* strong.
You're called to courage because *He's* present.

Whether you're:

- Leading a cabin devotion for the first time
- Correcting a camper's behavior
- Sharing your testimony
- Praying out loud in front of your team

- Talking to a camper about Jesus
- Or simply showing up when you feel completely inadequate

God is with you.

He's not calling you to be fearless. He's calling you to be *faithful*.

⚡ WHEN YOU FEEL THE FEAR, DO IT ANYWAY

Courage isn't the absence of fear. It's choosing to obey in spite of fear.

This summer, there will be moments when your heart races. Your voice shakes. You hesitate, wondering, *"Can I really do this?"*

And those moments matter.

Because that's where courage is born.

- When you feel unprepared—but you speak truth anyway.
- When you feel nervous—but you raise your hand to help.
- When you feel unsure—but you take the next step forward.

It's in those uncomfortable, awkward, uncertain spaces that God does some of His most beautiful work.

DON'T DOWNPLAY YOUR "YES"

It might seem silly to seasoned staffers that your first week made you nervous. Or that leading a prayer feels intimidating. Or that you're not used to being in charge of a group of kids.

But don't let comparison minimize your courage.

You have no idea what your obedience is setting in motion. You don't have to lead worship for twenty years to make a difference. Sometimes, the simple act of *showing up* and trusting God to use you *today* is the most courageous thing you'll do all summer.

 ## HOW TO LIVE WITH COURAGE AT CAMP

Here are a few ways to grow in courage this week:

1. START SMALL

Courage is a muscle. Start by taking one bold step each day—sharing a Scripture, volunteering to lead, or encouraging a teammate.

2. REMEMBER PAST VICTORIES

God has brought you through before. Look back at His faithfulness to move forward with confidence.

3. LEAN ON COMMUNITY

You don't have to be brave alone. Talk to a teammate. Ask for prayer. Courage grows in connection.

4. KEEP YOUR EYES ON JESUS

Fear shrinks when focus shifts. Fix your eyes not on the problem, but on the One who goes before you.

 **REFLECT**

Take a few moments today to reflect or journal on these:

- Where is God asking you to be courageous this summer?
- What fears are holding you back from stepping forward in faith?
- What might happen if you said "yes" anyway?

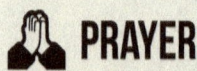 **PRAYER**

Father, thank You for being with me wherever I go. When I'm scared, uncertain, or overwhelmed, remind me that You are near. Give me the courage to obey You—whether it's leading, serving, speaking, or simply showing up. Let my small yes become something big in Your hands. I trust You to use me, stretch me, and grow me this summer. In Jesus' name, amen.

STAYING THE COURSE

Scripture – Deuteronomy 4:9 (ESV):
"Only take care, and keep your soul diligently, lest you forget the things that your eyes have seen, and lest they depart from your heart all the days of your life. Make them known to your children and your children's children..."

Camp doesn't last forever.

No matter how powerful the worship, how deep the conversations, how strong the connections—it all winds down. One day you'll pack your duffel bag, sweep out your cabin, say your goodbyes, and drive away.

The lake gets quiet. The dining hall echoes. The paths that were once crowded with laughter grow still.

And if you're not careful, you might start to think it was all temporary.
Just a season. Just a summer. Just a memory.

But let me remind you—*what God did here is not meant to stay here.*

 HOLY GROUND

I've had the gift of serving in camps for decades. I've seen the inside of cabins long forgotten, led worship at altars worn thin by tear-streaked prayers, and stood under the stars while dozens of students committed their lives to Christ.

My old camp director, Kendall Cameron, once described the campgrounds as *"holy ground."*

At first, I thought he just meant the chapel or the worship center—the "official" spiritual spaces. But over time, I began to understand what he really meant.

Holy ground isn't about stained glass or pews. It's any place where God moves, where hearts are changed, and where faith deepens. It's any space where heaven feels just a little closer to earth.

At camp, that might be:

- A fire circle where a camper whispered a prayer for the first time.
- A bunk bed where a counselor led someone to Jesus under the covers of darkness.
- A trail where God spoke during silent reflection.
- A morning devotion that cracked open a heart.
- A community of believers who carried each other through the hard days.

That's holy ground.

📑 REMEMBER WHAT YOU'VE SEEN

Deuteronomy 4:9 reminds us to *keep our soul diligently,* to not forget what our eyes have seen, and to hold onto what God has done.

Because life has a way of making us forget.

Back home, things get noisy. Schedules fill. Old habits creep back in. And the sacred things that happened at camp can start to fade.

But you don't have to lose them.
You can carry them with you.
You can remember.

- Remember the prayer you prayed at the altar.
- Remember the camper you loved with everything you had.
- Remember the breakthrough moment you never thought would come.
- Remember the friendships rooted in Scripture and forged in sweat.
- Remember how real God felt in the stillness of the woods, in the laughter of a cabin, in the pages of His Word.

These memories aren't sentimental—they're **spiritual anchors.**
They remind you who God is.
What He's done.
And what He *can still do.*

THE LASTING IMPACT

I'm old enough now to look back and see what camp did in the lives of so many I served with.

Dozens of pastors. Missionaries. Church leaders. Worship leaders. Camp directors. Teachers. Parents raising their own children in faith.

But I've also seen the other side.

Some who once stood at that same altar now walk in a different direction. Some who once prayed with passion now live with spiritual apathy. Their walk with Christ is cold—or gone.

Why the difference?

It's not always one choice. It's not always some dramatic fall. Often, it's just *forgetting*.

Forgetting what God did.
Forgetting who He is.
Forgetting that the call didn't end when camp did.

But you don't have to follow that path.

 ## KEEP YOUR SOUL DILIGENTLY

The summer may end.
The routine may change.
But the mission remains.

You are still called.

Still equipped.
Still part of the story God is writing.

Don't let this chapter close without asking God how He wants to use it in the next one.

What did He show you this summer?
What did He stir in you?
What are you carrying forward into your family, your church, your friendships, your future?

Your faith isn't confined to these campgrounds.
But this camp *can* be the launching pad for the rest of your walk with Jesus.

🌿 HOW TO STAY THE COURSE AFTER CAMP

So how do you keep your soul diligent? How do you hold on to what God has done here?

Here are a few simple rhythms that can help:

1. JOURNAL WHAT YOU'VE SEEN

Before you leave, write it down. The breakthroughs. The prayers. The names of campers. The Scriptures that spoke to you. Make a record of this holy ground.

2. STAY CONNECTED

Reach out to your fellow staff. Keep praying for your campers. Share updates. Iron sharpens iron—even after camp.

3. FIND A FAITH COMMUNITY

Get plugged into a local church or campus ministry. Don't drift. Anchor yourself with believers who will challenge and support you.

4. KEEP PRAYING

The God who met you at camp meets you in your bedroom. In your car. In your classroom. Stay close to Him through prayer.

5. SERVE SOMEWHERE

Don't wait for a position—find a need and meet it. Camp may be over, but ministry never stops.

⟳ A PLACE TO REMEMBER

Camp is sacred not just because of what happens here, but because of what it reminds us of:

- That God is near.
- That faith is real.
- That surrender is worth it.
- That your life has purpose.
- That community matters.
- That grace is always available.

So when your faith wavers—remember.
When the fire feels like it's fading—remember.
When you feel lost or stuck or small—remember.

Remember the God who met you here.
Remember the holy ground beneath your feet.
Remember the call to follow Him always.

 **REFLECT**

Take a few quiet moments to reflect or journal on these:

- What did God do in your heart this summer?
- Who impacted your faith the most, and why?
- How can you carry the lessons of camp into your everyday life?
- What will help you remember this season when you're tempted to forget?

 **PRAYER**

God, thank You for what You've done this summer. Thank You for meeting me here—for showing me Your faithfulness, Your love, and Your call. As I leave this place, help me not to forget. Keep my heart soft, my faith strong, and my eyes on You. Let this holy ground be a foundation I build my life on. Use everything I've experienced to shape who I become—for Your glory. In Jesus' name, amen.

🏕️ FINAL THOUGHTS: WHY AREN'T MORE PEOPLE BELIEVING?

Scripture – Romans 10:14 (ESV):
"How then will they call on him in whom they have not believed? And how are they to believe in him of whom they have never heard? And how are they to hear without someone preaching?"

After finishing this devotional, I thought I had written down all the stories that needed to be told—until one memory returned with such clarity that I knew it belonged here at the end.

It happened on the final night of camp.

The campers were in their bunks, the campfire was out, and the buzz of a long week had quieted. I turned out the cabin lights and, like I always did on Friday nights, stepped outside to sit under the stars. I had a stack of camper cards on my lap and a pen in hand—recording notes, stories, and reflections about the boys in my cabin. This was my chance to leave something helpful for future leaders and to pray over each name one last time.

I sat on a massive rock not far from the cabin, bathed in the soft glow of the moonlight. My heart was full. Tired, but full.

Then I heard footsteps on the path behind me.

It was Leonard—a quiet, thoughtful 12-year-old from my cabin.

A MOONLIT QUESTION

Leonard shuffled over and sat down near me. He looked up at the sky, then at me, and said,

"Did Jesus really love me? And how can I follow Him?"

No loud music. No crowd. No altar call. Just a boy with questions under a blanket of stars.

I set the cards aside, turned toward him, and answered the best I could. Slowly. Simply. Carefully. We talked about who Jesus is. What He had done. Why it mattered. And I asked Leonard what he wanted to do with what he now understood.

"I want to follow Him," he said. "I want to believe in Jesus."

So we prayed.

Right there under the stars, Leonard became a new creation in Christ. I watched a child walk into the Kingdom of God— and all I could do was thank God for letting me be a part of it.

A QUESTION THAT STILL ECHOES

After we finished praying, Leonard stood up, started walking back to the cabin, then turned around and asked a question I still can't shake:

"Why aren't more people believing in Jesus?"

It was innocent. Honest. Pure.

But it struck me like lightning.

Why *aren't* they?

Leonard wasn't questioning Jesus—he was questioning *us*. And the answer I've come to embrace over the years is painfully simple:

Too often, we're not telling them.

THE MISSION DOESN'T END HERE

Camp is powerful. But it's not the end goal.

It's *training ground*.
It's *holy ground*.
It's where you learn to see people like Jesus sees them.
It's where you learn to speak truth with love.
It's where you find the courage to share, the wisdom to listen, and the faith to follow wherever God leads you next.

The Great Commission wasn't just given to pastors or missionaries.
It was given to *us all*.

"Go therefore and make disciples of all nations..." (Matthew 28:19)

And if you've ever told a camper about Jesus...
If you've ever led a devotion, or prayed with someone, or modeled love when it was hard...
You've already *started*.

 ## YOU ARE A WITNESS

God used camp to shape me—and not just as a counselor, but as a believer, a leader, a man, a husband, and a dad.

I've seen the ripple effects of summer staff stretch into pulpits, youth groups, mission fields, classrooms, and homes. I've also seen hearts grow cold when camp becomes a memory instead of a mission.

Leonard's question is still echoing.

And it demands a response—not just from me, but from you.

Will you stay the course?
Will you keep sharing?
Will you remember the holy ground beneath your feet this summer—and carry that same spirit wherever God sends you next?

 ## LIVING WHAT YOU'VE LEARNED

As you leave camp and return to "normal" life, here are a few ways to keep the mission alive:

KEEP SHARING YOUR FAITH

Don't overcomplicate it. Just be honest, kind, and bold. Tell people what Jesus has done for you.

BE READY FOR THE LEONARDS

They're everywhere—at your school, your job, your church, even in your family. Keep your eyes open and your heart soft.

WRITE IT DOWN

Journal the moments that mattered most. Mark what God did this summer. Return to them when your faith feels weak.

STAY IN COMMUNITY

Surround yourself with people who challenge you to keep growing. Don't walk alone.

KEEP THE FIRE GOING

The mountaintop moments don't have to fade. Stay in the Word. Keep praying. Worship often. Live faithfully.

 **REFLECT**

Take some quiet time today to reflect or journal:

- Who is your "Leonard"? Who might God be placing in your path?
- How has your perspective on your role as a disciple changed this summer?
- What will it take for you to live out your calling after camp?

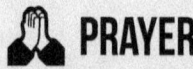 **PRAYER**

Jesus, thank You for Leonard. Thank You for his honesty, his courage, and his new life in You. Let me never forget the moment You changed his heart. I pray that I would have the same boldness—to keep sharing, keep loving, and keep living on mission. Use me beyond camp. Let this summer mark the beginning, not the end. Send me out, Lord, as Your witness. In Your name, amen.

ABOUT THE AUTHOR

James McLamb is a passionate communicator, youth advocate, and founder of Generation Youth. With a unique blend of classroom experience and entrepreneurial leadership, James has dedicated his life to equipping and inspiring the next generation. His work is deeply influenced by the legacy of Zig Ziglar, blending timeless values with real-world strategies to help young people thrive.

James is the creator of the Generation Youth Coaching Certification, a powerful program designed to equip educators, life coaches, and leaders to effectively mentor and empower youth. His practical, heart-led approach has made him one of the nation's go-to experts in youth development.

A former high school agriculture teacher, James holds degrees from North Carolina State University and Clemson University in Agricultural Education and Youth Development Leadership. He's the author of *Tomorrow's Youth* and host of The Generation Youth Podcast, where he shares stories, insights, and tools to help young people grow in confidence and purpose.

James lives in North Carolina with his wife of 30 years, Melissa, and their three children—Sara Beth, Jacob, and Abby.

To connect with James or invite him to speak at your event, reach out at james@generationziglar.com.

YOU WERE MADE TO MAKE A DIFFERENCE!

Step into your calling to impact the next generation with purpose, clarity, and confidence.

The **Generation Youth Life Coaching Certification** equips adults to guide young people through life's most defining challenges:

- Mindset
- Self-Image
- Relationships
- Goal-Setting

You'll gain:

- ☑ A powerful 12-session coaching curriculum
- ☑ A complete Coaches' Guide and Youth Client Manual
- ☑ Step-by-step guidance to create your *own* coaching content

☑ In-depth training on what it truly means to be a youth life coach

☑ Live and virtual training experiences

☑ A supportive, connected community of coaches and leaders

Whether you're a parent, teacher, mentor, or youth camp counselor, or simply someone who wants to make a lasting difference, this certification gives you the tools to lead with wisdom, purpose, and heart.

Because youth coaching is too important to do alone—and your influence matters more than ever.

Learn more and apply today at ☞generation-youth.com